12/00

Book
Written
Prior to 10/19/06
M

Tractor-Trailer
Trucker

A Powerful Truck Book

Tractor-Trailer
Trucker

A Powerful Truck Book

Joyce Slayton Mitchell

Photographs by Steven Borns

Tricycle Press
Berkeley, California

To Sawyer Jarzyna Connelly,

best neighbor and favorite third grader.

—J.S.M.

To Lawrence William, father;

Lawrence Patrick, brother-in-law;

and Lawrence Gilbert, nephew.

—S.B.

Sources and Acknowledgements

For teaching us everything we know about trucking, we would like to thank the following people: Joe Bellavance, president of A. Bellavance Trucking, Inc.; his son, operations manager Roland Bellavance, who so generously gave his time and expertise, and allowed us access to others in his company; dispatchers David Bellavance and Richard Dufresne; Ann M. Wakefield, resource librarian of the American Trucking Association; Mary Venditta, of Corporate Affairs of Mack Trucks; and Nick Robinson, driver for Yellow Freight System, Inc. We are especially grateful to tractor-trailer trucker Ken Blair of Hardwick, Vermont, and want to acknowledge his professionalism and dedication to a 3-million-mile, 30-year career of life on the road. We thank him for generously sharing 6,703 miles of it with photographer Steven Borns.

Finally, we want to enthusiastically express our appreciation to Tricycle Press publisher Nicole Geiger and editor Cybele Knowles for providing their editorial guidance and a teamwork environment for this exciting project: *Tractor-Trailer Trucker*.

UNDER THE HOOD

Before starting out, check oil, water, and coolant levels. Check hoses and fan belts. When the belts are new, check for tightness. As belts get older, check for cracks, fraying, and slackness.

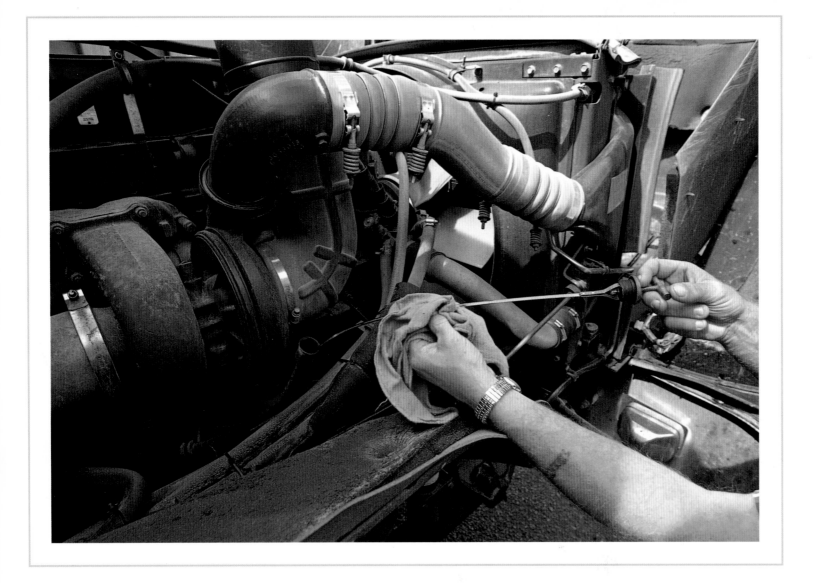

OIL AND WATER

Check oil level with the dipstick. The oil must be changed every 20,000 miles. If the engine starts to overheat due to oil or water leaks while you are driving, a warning light on your control panel will come on. You then have 30 to 40 seconds to find a safe parking spot before the engine automatically shuts down as a safety measure.

CHECK THE SHOCKS

The shock absorber is under the fifth wheel of the tractor. Check shock absorber mounts and the mounting eyes at each end of the shock. Look for fluid leakage: check for oil stains on the sides of the shock absorber tubes.

HOOK UP TRACTOR AND TRAILER

Make sure fifth-wheel jaws are open. Back tractor as squarely as possible at the center of the trailer until fifth-wheel jaws engage the kingpin on the trailer. Check that fifth-wheel jaws have closed completely around trailer kingpin. Make sure that no daylight shows between the fifth wheel and the trailer's deck plate. Perform a pull test—pulling forward with the trailer brakes set—to check the coupling.

HOOK UP LIGHT LINE AND BRAKE LINES

Hook up trailer light line and brake lines, and check connections for air leaks on the brake lines. Secure lines properly to prevent tangling or chafing.

LOAD

Load cargo at the warehouse, and then check in with the dispatcher for trucking orders.

CHAINS AND STRAPS

Carry extra chains and straps, since cargo can shift during the long drive. The storage rack holds 2-inch straps, 4-inch straps, chains, ratchet binders, winch binders, bungees, and felt and plastic corner protectors.

TRACTOR-TRAILER TIRES

Good tires help you steer well and support the heavy weight of the load. Measure the depth of the tire tread with a tire-depth gauge, or for a quick check, use a dime. New tires have a tread of $18/32$ of an inch. When the front tire treads get worn down to $4/32$ of an inch, tires must be changed. Change tires after 100,000 to 120,000 miles.

AIRBAGS

Check airbags under trailer for visual signs of damage. Airbags balance the cargo load and make the trailer weight even for a smooth and safe ride.

THREE-POINT STANCE

Be sure of foothold and handhold when entering and exiting the cab. Use a three-point stance: two feet on the steps and one hand on the handhold. Remember that steps, handhold, gratings, and fuel tank tops can be extra slippery when oily.

GEARS

There are 8 to 18 gears in an 18-wheeler. This tractor has 13 gears. Gears 1 to 5 are the low gears, and 6 to 13 are the high gears.

Move the stick shift to change from gear to gear. Press the black button on the stick shift to change from the low gears to the high gears. Within the high gears, press the red button (the split-switcher) to shift half a gear. Select gear 13 to cruise at the speed limit on interstate highways.

START ENGINE AND CHECK EMERGENCY EQUIPMENT

Start engine and set at low idle for warm-up. Check for abnormal engine noise. Check gauges for normal readings. Check horns and windshield wipers pre-trip and post-trip. Check steering-wheel action. Test all lights, including four-way flasher switch for turn signals.

CHECK AIR BRAKES

Put trailer air supply valve in "normal." Step on brake pedal to apply and release brakes. Pump brakes and check readings. A normal reading is 90 to 120 pounds per square inch (psi). When the air pressure falls below 60 psi, "low air" warnings will activate and all brakes will automatically lock as a safety measure.

Drive.

FILL UP

Each fuel tank holds 100 to 150 gallons. There are two tanks on an 18-wheeler. Check both tanks every day. Big tractor-trailers get 5.5 miles per gallon.

SATELLITE PAGING

Use satellite paging system to check schedule and destination goals.

SLEEPER

The sleeper can be as big as 340 cubic feet of space (up to 8 feet high and 6 feet, 2 inches deep). The biggest sleepers have room for a bed, refrigerator, TV, VCR, microwave, laptop computer, storage space for clothes, sink, and toilet. Some of the biggest sleepers even have room for two bunk beds. Park at a truck stop or rest area to sleep.

TRUCK STOP

Take time out for breakfast at the truck stop. Truck stops are convenient places to shower and eat.

CB RADIO

Use the citizens band (CB) radio to talk to other truckers about traffic conditions and weather reports. The trucker's CB radio channel is #19. The emergency channel is #9.

On the road again...

Trucker Talk

anchor it: apply brakes for an emergency stop

barefoot: crossing a mountain pass without chains on the tires

hammer down: move fast, foot to the floor

roll and rest: when a long-haul driver drives and stops to sleep at regular intervals

gear bonger: trucker who grinds gears when shifting

chicken coop: weigh station

flip-flop: U-turn

monkey pickles: bananas (dark green when shipped)

backhaul: return load. After delivering a load of cargo, the trucker usually picks up another load that needs to be delivered somewhere close to headquarters.

motion lotion: diesel fuel, also called "go juice"

double nickel: 55 miles per hour

alligator: big hunk of rubber tread peeled off a truck tire, found on the side of the road

bark from the stacks: backfire from muffler

grunt for the grades: enough horsepower to get up steep hills with a heavy load

hundred-mile coffee: very strong coffee

bobtail: a tractor only, no trailer

covered wagon: trailer with sides and tarp

wiggle wagon: a tractor pulling double or triple trailers

skateboard: flatbed trailer

shiny hiney: trailer with stainless steel back door (Truckers don't drive close to these at night because headlights reflect back brightly.)

big rig: tractor-trailer

eighteen-wheeler: tractor-trailer with 18 wheels

four-wheeler: car

kiddie car: school bus

smoke him: pass another vehicle

bird dog: radar detector

coffin: sleeper compartment in the tractor

pigtail: light line used to transmit electrical power to trailer

break the unit: unhitch the tractor from the trailer

jump the pin: miss the kingpin when hitching tractor and trailer

10-4: "yes" or "OK" on the CB radio

10-20: trucker's location ("What's your 10-20?")

10-33: traffic due to accidents, natural disasters, and emergency vehicles such as ambulances and fire trucks

10-36: a call for the correct time ("What's the 10-36?")

ratchet jaw: trucker who talks too much on the CB

mud duck: very weak radio signal

brush your teeth and comb your hair: be on best driving behavior and within speed limit, because state trooper is approaching

bear: state trooper, also called "Smokey Bear"

bear bait: anyone driving over the speed limit

bear bite: a speeding ticket

feed the bears: pay a speeding ticket

bear den: state trooper station or headquarters

bear in the air: helicopter highway patrol, also called "spy in the sky"

bear in the bushes: state trooper hiding with a radar gun

front door: in front of the truck, as in "You've got a bear's den about two miles on your front door"

back door: behind the truck, as in "You've got a bear on your back door"

Glossary

air supply valve: controls air pressure for brakes

brake lines: air cords that run from tractor to trailer for operating trailer brakes

coolant: liquid that flows through the radiator to keep the engine cool

corner protector: felt or plastic guards that prevent damage to straps and cargo

deck plate: steel pad that provides a flat surface for the fifth-wheel hitch

dipstick: metal rod for measuring engine oil level

fan belt: turns the fan to cool the radiator

fifth wheel: hitch on tractor used to connect trailer

fifth-wheel jaws: moving parts of tractor hitch that open and close around kingpin

high gears: cruising gears

idle: speed of engine while truck is at rest

kingpin: metal pin on the trailer that fifth-wheel jaws enclose

landing gear: support for trailer when parked without tractor

light line: cord that conducts electricity from tractor to trailer for operating trailer lights

low gears: starting gears

post-trip: after finishing a work day

pre-trip: before starting a work day

ratchet binder: tool used to tighten chains

satellite paging: provides email between truckers and their headquarters

shock absorber: smoothes out vertical motion. "Shocks" look like metal tubes with flat pieces of metal (mounts) with a hole (eye) at each end to bolt shock absorber to cab.

tractor: vehicle that pulls the trailer

trailer: unit attached to the tractor; holds cargo

trucking orders: trip instructions issued by dispatcher

winch binder: tool used to tighten straps

Tricycle Press
P.O. Box 7123
Berkeley, CA 94707
www.tenspeed.com

Design by Catherine Jacobes
Typeset in Serpentine Sans and Franklin Gothic

Library of Congress Cataloging-in-Publication Data

Mitchell, Joyce Slayton.
    Tractor-trailer trucker: a powerful truck book / by Joyce Slayton Mitchell; photographs by Steven Borns.
        p. cm.
    Summary: Introduces the various parts of a tractor trailer and their functions as a truck driver prepares to take his "big rig" on the road.
    ISBN 1-58246-010-8
    1. Tractor trailer combinations Juvenile literature.
    2. Truck driving Juvenile literature. [1. Tractor trailers. 2. Trucks.]
    I. Borns, Steven, ill. II. Title.
TL230.15.M58   2000
629.2844—dc21   99-38509
                                        CIP

First printing, 2000
Printed in China

2 3 4 5 6 – 04 03 02 01 00

Check out these websites for more information about trucks:
www.homeroad.com
www.nozone.org